Avery Coonley house, Riverside, Ill.

THE EARLY WORK OF
FRANK LLOYD WRIGHT
The "Ausgeführte Bauten" of 1911

With a New Introduction by
Grant Carpenter Manson

DOVER PUBLICATIONS, INC.
NEW YORK

Unity Temple, Oak Park, Ill.

Published in Canada by General Publishing Company, Ltd., 30 Lesmill Road, Don Mills, Toronto, Ontario.
Published in the United Kingdom by Constable and Company, Ltd., 10 Orange Street, London WC2H 7EG.

This Dover edition, first published in 1982, is a republication of *Frank Lloyd Wright: Ausgeführte Bauten* as published by Ernst Wasmuth, Berlin, in 1911. In the present edition the original introduction "Frank Lloyd Wright. Eine Studie zu seiner Würdigung," by C. R. Ashbee, has been replaced by a new introduction by Grant Carpenter Manson, captions have been translated into English, and a glossary of German terms found in the ground plans has been added. The drawing reproduced above originally appeared, lightly tinted in color, on the inside front cover of the Wasmuth edition.

Manufactured in the United States of America
Dover Publications, Inc., 180 Varick Street, New York, N.Y. 10014

Library of Congress Cataloging in Publication Data

Wright, Frank Lloyd. 1867–1959.
The early work of Frank Lloyd Wright-The "Ausgeführte Bauten" of 1911.

English and German.
Originally published: Ausgeführte Bauten. Berlin : E. Wasmuth, 1911. With translations of captions and a glossary of German words on floor plans.
1. Wright, Frank Lloyd. 1867–1959. I. Title. II. Title: "Ausgeführte Bauten" of 1911.
NA737.W7A4 1982   720'.924   82-9437
ISBN 0-486-24381-8 (pbk.)   AACR2

Introduction to the
Dover Edition

by Grant Carpenter Manson

The book presents, in the form of a photograph album, the major completed works of Frank Lloyd Wright's Oak Park Period.

The Oak Park Period . . . what an evocative phrase! It stands for, and is synchronous with, the first third of the Master's career, 1893 to 1910. It is a period during which Wright brought forth and materialized all the basic elements of that extraordinary principle of architectural design which lay, awaiting expression, across the lobes of his brain. Indeed, the period is so fundamental to the career, so all-embracing, that it is entirely possible that, had the career terminated in 1910 instead of merely reaching a pause, Wright's place in the story of the emergence of modern architecture would be no less defined and no less secure.[1]

The present reprint of *Frank Lloyd Wright: Ausgeführte Bauten* (Wasmuth, Berlin, 1911) brings to view again the first real panorama of what these years were all about. It is made up largely of the photographs of Henry Fuermann,[2] who, like other artists and craftspersons who form the shadowy background of those years, touched, in the contact with Wright, the perimeters of enduring fame. Together, the photographs constitute in visual terms the original announcement to the world, in these pristine seventeen years of Wright's development, of what architecture meant to him, both in its domestic and public aspects. They run the gamut from Unity Temple and the Larkin Headquarters Building to what is perhaps the central jewel of the accomplishment, the celebrated prairie house.

That the first full-scale publicity accorded Wright should have originated in Germany, while explicable, is startlingly curious. It derives from the fact that advanced taste in metropolitan Germany, in the opening decade of this century, had succumbed to the attractions of Jugendstil, Sezession, and Arts and Crafts. Men like Joseph Maria Olbrich, Koloman Moser and Bruno Paul on the Continent, and Charles Francis Voysey and Charles Rennie Mackintosh in Britain were lionized, while the fashionable suburbs of southwest Berlin, for example, were a showcase of what these men and movements had to offer in domestic architecture and applied design. Somehow, what wisps of information about Oak Park had reached the German avant-garde misled it into classifying Wright with the European designers of the moment who were uppermost in its mind, and the moment, as Wasmuth and his text writer C. R. Ashbee realized, was ripe for confrontation and clarification. Thus, the curiosity: Wright's debut as an international figure took place in Berlin, where it was quickly seen that the new transatlantic phenomenon was no Paul, no Voysey. In applied design he was perhaps their equal—in architecture he was astronomically more.

There is paradox in this chain of events. There is virtually no trace of Jugendstil or Art Nouveau in Wright; the linkage to Arts and Crafts is superficial. Then, we may ask, since Wright was his own man, how did he come to find himself making his bow in this cast of characters—*dans cette galère?*

As has been intimated, Wright had been granted little publicity prior to 1910, and certainly none of the caliber which would be given dissemination abroad. The one exception was the generous and perspicacious article by a fellow Chicagoan: Robert C. Spencer, Jr.'s "The Work of Frank Lloyd Wright" in the June 1900 edition of *Architectural Review* (Boston). As its title

---

[1] I said something along these lines at the close of my book *Frank Lloyd Wright to 1910: The First Golden Age*, Reinhold, New York, 1958. This book and this article are necessarily interrelated.

[2] Fuermann was the Chicago architectural photographer whom Wright commissioned from time to time during the Oak Park Period to make visual records of his completed designs. Fuermann worked with wet-plate glass negatives, unfortunately fragile. Many of them are irretrievably lost, no doubt broken. There is a colorful rumor, revealing the extent to which Wright, after the 1909–14 irregularities, had fallen into oblivion in Chicagoland, that bushel-basketfuls of these glass negatives found their way into the local greenhouse-construction industry.

Unity Temple under construction, 1908.

implies, its coverage was, to date, comprehensive. It was read on both sides of the Atlantic. It was, to be sure, a narrow sample, only just nicking into the second decade of Oak Park, but it was enough to start the ball rolling. One European who was struck by it was C. R. Ashbee, Fellow of the Royal British Institute of Architects and leading light in the British Arts and Crafts Movement. Thoroughly grounded in the polite architecture of his time, he was also sensitive to the aims of William Morris and his followers. Ashbee was thus in a position to evaluate what was passing in those years in America as first-rate architecture—the work of the great firms and Beaux-Arts practitioners of the eastern seaboard—and, in contrast, the work of the gifted mavericks Henry Hobson Richardson, Frank Furness, Louis Sullivan et al. And now, thanks to Spencer, here was this young man Wright out in Illinois hitting the press with something quite revolutionary. If, on the surface, there was a suggestion of Morris and Voysey, of Arts and Crafts, in inner meaning it was light-years beyond such amiable superficialities. At four thousand miles' distance, it was hard to tell: one must go and *look*. Presently he was in Oak Park, being led by Jane

Addams, Wright tells us in *An Autobiography*, to the door of the Studio on the leafy corner of Chicago and Forest Avenues. The tradition of The Pilgrimage had, so early, begun.

The other European who now caught vibrations from Oak Park was the German educationist Kuno Francke, holder in the academic year 1908–09 of a

Model of Unity Temple.

visiting lectureship in aesthetics at Harvard University. During this year, he, like Ashbee, traveled to the Studio for a closer look at the man and the place from which these vibrations were emanating. The coming together of Wright and Francke was a warm and rewarding experience for both men. They were simpatico. Francke was undisguisedly affected by what he learned and saw, whereas Wright, flattered by the attention and giving rein to his Germanophilia (a lifetime characteristic, albeit of uncertain origin), put forth his beguiling best. Upon his return to Germany, Francke wasted no time in passing on to Ernst Wasmuth, the Berlin arbiter and publisher of developments in the world of architecture, the import of what he had seen, fortifying lines of information that had already reached him via Ashbee. That here was an opportunity to launch a new architectural star in orbit was not lost. Wasmuth decided to be the first to publish Wright in Europe. The result was the now-famous duo: the two-volume elephant folio *Frank Lloyd Wright: Ausgeführte Bauten und Entwürfe,* Wasmuth, Berlin, 1910, and *Frank Lloyd Wright: Ausgeführte Bauten,* Wasmuth, Berlin, 1911. The first consists of a selection of presentation and working drawings, in loose leaf, of both executed and unexecuted designs, without text but with a catalogue raisonné in a separate insert, covering Wright's career from inception to date. To make and/or assemble these scores of magnificent drawings, the entire staff at the Studio had labored for untold months. To find one of these monumental sets today, complete and in fair condition, is a search for a new Button Gwinnett signature—always possible, but highly unlikely. The second Wasmuth publication, made up of a single slender volume, is the publication with which we are here concerned. Ashbee supplied the Introduction (translated into German); there is no other text. Simpler in format as well as more compact in span, it concerns itself with, as the title states, only those designs which were executed. This book is essentially a photograph album; the only drawings are the working plans for each structure.

It was the final (really last-minute) editing of these works-in-progress, seemingly so crucial to his success, that drew Wright to Berlin in the autumn of 1909, at the time of his flight from Oak Park in company with Mamah Borthwick Cheney, the first woman with whom he was to become extramaritally—and, ultimately, tragically—involved. This event wrote an abrupt and final *finis* to the first third of his sixty-year career, and to the Oak Park Period.

This book spans in photographs the executed productions of the Oak Park Period. Not only does it include all the great commissions—the landmarks along the way that we could expect to find in any anthology of Wright's early work—but also many lesser-known

Terra-cotta figure at the entrance to the Dana house. Frank Lloyd Wright, architect, Richard Bock, sculptor.

commissions in domestic and interior design which serve to round out the picture of what was on the drafting tables and in the minds of Wright and his cohorts at the Studio in these seminal years. It should also be stressed that these photographs, as essential records, preserve for us in simulacrum the buildings that were, like the Larkin Building, subsequently demolished, and the buildings that, although still standing, have been the victims of the simple wear-and-tear of time or of unfortunate attempts in later years to "improve" them, or of attempts to bring them up to subsequent underwriters' standards, as in the case of the Winslow House, where the roofing material—hand-built pantiles—was replaced by asbestos shingles, with indescribably coarsening effect.

The arrangement within the book of the designs presented may at first glance seem arbitrary, but there is some broad organization. The book opens and closes with the two great public commissions of the period: Unity and Larkin. These hold within bookends, as it were, an impressive march-past of private houses, plus a few shops, exhibition rooms, and set pieces thrown in for flavor. The occasional introduction of trivia—items of furniture Niedecken-built to Studio specifications, favorite statues in plaster cast and bits of Studio bric-a-brac, panels inscribed with Elbert Hubbard mottoes, pots of dried leaves and sumac gathered from the vacant lots to the west of the Studio and along the Desplaines River—can be viewed nostalgically as endearing evidence of some of the enthusiasms which

these talented people in America's age of innocence shared. It took some kind of glue to hold them together so long, despite racking dissensions.

There is, as this layout must reveal, no attempt to present the material chronologically, and it is this which gives the random note. Where the private houses are concerned, the scheme has serious faults; we will touch upon these shortly. But, looking at Wright's early work altogether in this way, something informative does emerge. What we have here is a ringing declaration of independence from old ways of perceiving the art of architecture. We are told, as we open the book and again as we close it, that space in public buildings dedicated to congregations of people must, as a countereffect, have self-containment (an almost classic unity), must be primarily top-lighted, and must be kept in place by complex, hardworking structural surrounds. Then, in the middle passages of the book, we are told that, in buildings where people *live*, space must be a free horizontal flow through the fabric of the structure with ribbons of light on its perimeters. This shift in rationale is a compelling testimony. We realize that we are observing the workings of an unfettered mind addressing itself *de novo* to the central problem of manmade structures: the mass-space relationship.

In his introduction to the 1911 edition, and in an attempt to explain all this profound originality, Ashbee makes a demographic approach: this new architecture is arising in a new land; it is a response, like the songs of Walt Whitman, by gifted native sons to an exhila-

Entrance to the Dana House, Springfield, Ill.

Coonley villa,
Riverside, Ill.

Coonley villa, Riverside, Ill.

rating set of new conditions. True, no doubt—and we remember that Wright always was a self-aware and self-proclaiming native son. But, in his case, it is only partial truth. "Crossing the Brooklyn Ferry" may offer a clue to the part that sheer freedom played in the American phenomenon, but, when applied to Frank Lloyd Wright, it only begins to answer the question "Why?" There is something other than ambience, something, as I tried to argue in my previously cited book, that came from *within*.

Influences were brought to bear, of course, upon innate, private conviction. The wonderful cubes and prisms of Unity and Larkin are crystallizations of ideas planted in Wright's mind by the Froebel "gifts" to which he was introduced as a child. The elegant, cultivated horizontal line of the prairie house was suggested by the precedent of Japanese traditional wooden architecture.. But to whom, other than himself, did Wright owe, for a start, the idea of the "first modern church in the world"—Unity Temple, 1906—stripped

Panel, Larkin Building. Frank Lloyd Wright, architect, Richard Bock, sculptor.

7

of all expected churchly trappings and made *(horribile dictu)* of cast concrete? To whom, other than himself, did he owe the concept of a dwelling—Robie House, 1908[3]—as a structure scaled down to its human occupants and in which the horizontal flow of unobstructed space was as paramount to its design as the daily ebb and flow of human activity within it?

This latter consideration prompts me to recommend, as a conducted experiment in how it came about, juxta-posing four houses of the Oak Park Period: Winslow (pp. 18 and 19), Heurtley (pp. 86–89), Willits (pp. 56–59) and Robie (pp. 112–115). Viewing them in a chronological order makes clear the wondrous unfolding, within little more than a single decade, of this revolutionary vision of that most basic fabrication of mankind: the dwelling. And here I return to my earlier-stated objection to the random make-up of this volume: it would have been more valuable to the student of Wright's early work had it been arranged chronologically. Nonetheless, the book's present rebirth in facsimile is welcome, as is anything that helps to illuminate and, if possible, to explain, the miracle of Wright's architecture.

---

[3]Records show that Robie House was completed in 1908, not 1906, the date given in this volume. The book is, in fact, alive with mistaken datings. As a facsimile reprint, these mistakes are left here as they are. The reader is hereby put on warning to check, if he is interested, every date he sees.

Glossary of German Words Found in the Ground Plans

Ab: down.
Abhang: slope.
Absatz: landing.
Abzug: sink.
Alkoven: alcoves.
Angestellte: employees.
Ankleidezimmer: dressing room.
Anrichtezimmer: pantry.
Arbeitzimmer: study, workroom.
Atelier: studio.
Auf: up.
Aufbewahrungsort: depository.
Ausgang: exit.

Bach: brook.
Bächlein: rivulet.
Bad: bath, bathroom.
Balkon: balcony.
Balkongeschoss(es): balcony floor.
Bedeckt(er): covered.
Bedeckte Laube: pergola.
Bedienten: servants.
Bibliothek: library.
Billiardzimmer: billiard room.
Blumen: flowers.
Blumengarten: flower garden.
Bowling Spielplatz: bowling alley.
Brücke: bridge.
Bücher: books.
Bureau (Büro): office.

Cassirer (Kassierer): cashier.
Chor: choir.
Closet (Klosett): lavatory.
Coje (Koje): stand, stall.
Corridor (Korridor): corridor.

Dach: roof.
Dachgarten: roof garden.
Deckfenster: skylight.
Diener: servant.
Dienerin: maid.
Dienerinzimmer: maid's room.
Diensthof: servants' yard.
Druckerei: print room or shop.

Eigenes Zimmer: owner's room.
Eintritts Halle: entrance hall.
Eis: ice.
Eltern: parents.
Empfangszimmer: reception room.
Entwurfszimmer: drafting room.
Erdengeschoss(es): ground floor.
Erhaben(er): raised.
Exhedra: exedra.

Fahreintritt: drive entrance.
Fahrräder: bicycles.
Fahrstuhl: elevator.

Fahrweg: driveway.
Feuerfest(es): fireproof.
Feuerraum: furnace.
Frauen: ladies.
Frühstück: breakfast (room).
Fundament: basement.
Futter Raum: feed room.

Galerie: gallery.
Garage: garage.
Garderobe: checkroom, wardrobe.
Garten: garden.
Gärtnerhäuschen: gardener's cottage.
Gast: guest.
Gehege: enclosure.
Gewölbe: vaulted area.
Grundriss: ground plan.

Halbgrundriss: half ground plan.
Halbkreis: semicircle.
Halle: hall.
Hauptgeschoss(es): main floor.
Haus: house.
Hausmeister: caretaker.
Heizkörper: radiator.
Hinter: rear.
Hof: yard, court.
Höherer Teil: upper portion.
Hörsaal: auditorium.
Hühner: chickens.

Im Freien: outdoor(s).
In (im): in.

Kanzel: pulpit.
Keller: cellar.
Kinder: children.
Kinderstube: nursery.
Klavier: piano.
Kleider: clothes (closet).
Kloster: cloister.
Korridor: corridor.
Küche: kitchen.
Kühlraum: refrigeration room.
Kuhst. (Kuhstall): cowshed.
Kutscher: carriages.

Laube: see bedeckte Laube.
Lageplan: plan of site.
Licht: light.
Lichtschacht: light well.
Leinen: linen (closet).
Loggia: loggia.

Mädchen: maid.
Männer: men.
Möbel: furniture.
Musik: music.

Nähstube: sewing room.

Ober: upper.
Oberlicht: skylight.
Offen: open.
Orgel: organ.
Orgelzimmer: organ loft.

Pavillon: pavilion.
Pfarrer: minister.
Porte cochere: porte cochere.

Rasenplatz: lawn.
Raum: room.
Restaurant: restaurant.

Schlafzimmer: bedroom.
Schräg: slanting, sloping, inclined.
Schrank: closet.
Schrankzimmer: locker room.
Sind: there are.
Sitz: seat.
Sitzkasten: window seat, settle.
Sonntagschule: Sunday school.
Speise Tisch: dining table.
Speisezimmer: dining room.
Stall: stall.
Stall Hof: stable yard.
Strasse: street.

Teich: pool.
Telefon: telephone.
Telefonzelle: telephone booth.
Terrasse: terrace.
Tisch: table.
Toiletten: toilets.
Treppe: steps, stairs.
Typisch(en): typical.

Und: and.
Unterhaltung: maintenance (area).

Veranda: veranda.
Versenkt(er): sunken.
Vestibül: vestibule.
Viertelgrundriss: quarter ground plan.
Vorbau: porch.
Vorfahrt: driveway.
Vorrat: store, stock, supply.
Vorzimmer: anteroom.

Wäscherei: laundry room.
Waschraum: toilet.
Werkstatt: workshop.
Wohnung: house, residence, dwelling, living quarters.
Wohnungs Saal: reception room.
Wohnzimmer: living room.

z.: see Zimmer or zu.
Zimmer: room.
Zu (zum, zur): to.
Zwischenstock(es): mezzanine.

Unity Temple, Oak Park, Ill.

Unity Temple and Unity House. Oak Park, Ill.

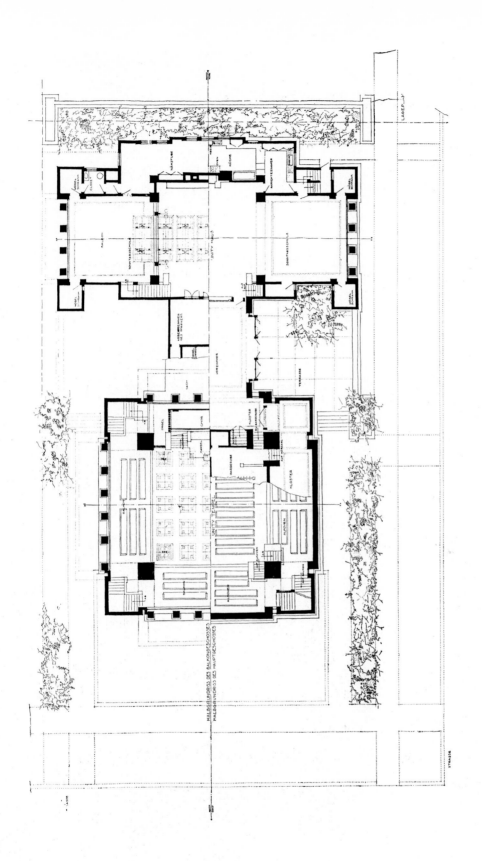

Unity Temple and Unity House. Ground plan.

Unity Temple and Unity House, Oak Park, Ill.

ABOVE: Unity Temple, west facade. BELOW: Unity House, west facade.

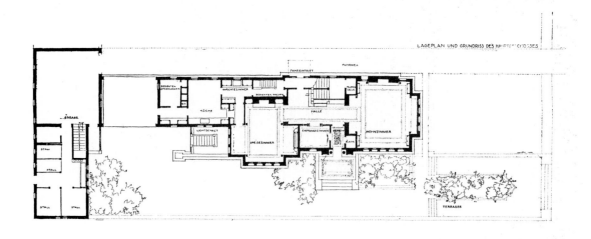

ABOVE: Interior of Unity Temple. BELOW: Isidor Heller house, Chicago.
   Ground plan.

City residence of Isidor Heller, Woodlawn Avenue, Chicago, 1896.

W. H. Winslow house, River Forest, Ill. Entrance and ground plan.

W. H. Winslow house, River Forest, 1893.

Husser villa, Buena Park, Chicago, 1898.

Husser villa, Chicago. West and south facades.

Williams villa, River Forest, Ill., 1894.

B. Harley Bradley house, Kankakee, Ill., 1900.

Bradley house, Kankakee, Ill. Entranceway and dining room.

Bradley house, Kankakee, Ill. Living room.

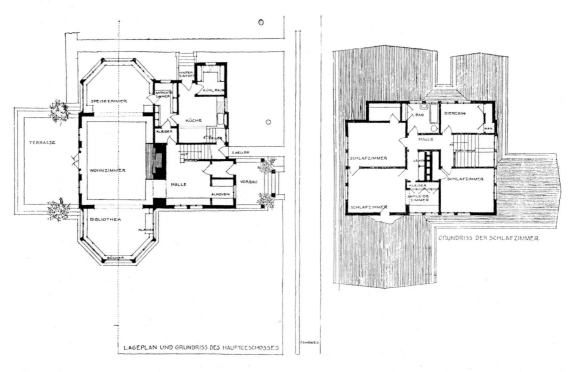

Warren Hickox house, Kankakee, Ill., 1900. South facade and ground plan.

Warren Hickox house, Kankakee, Ill. East facade.

Thomas house, Oak Park, Ill., 1902.

Thomas house, Oak Park, Ill. Details of the east facade.

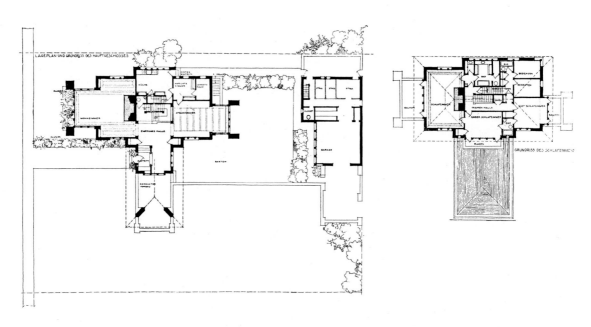

Country house of F. W. Little, Peoria, Ill., 1900.

Country house of F. W. Little, Peoria, Ill.

Susan L. Dana house, Springfield, Ill., 1899.

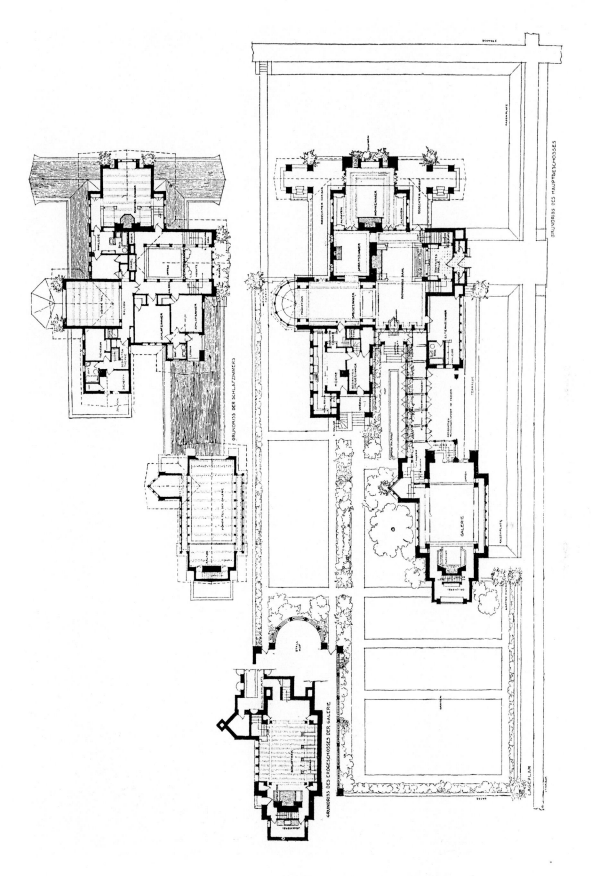

Susan L. Dana house, Springfield, Ill. Ground plans of the main and upper
floors.

33

Dana house, Springfield, Ill. South facade.

Dana house, Springfield, Ill. Details of the entrance facade.

Dana house, Springfield, Ill. Dining room.

Dana house, Springfield, Ill. Fountain in the dining room.

Dana house, Springfield, Ill. Details of the dining room and breakfast niche.

Dana house, Springfield, Ill. East facade.

Dana house, Springfield, Ill. East facade.

Dana house, Springfield, Ill. Double door and gallery.

Dana house, Springfield, Ill. Exterior of the gallery.

Dana house, Springfield, Ill. Interior of the gallery.

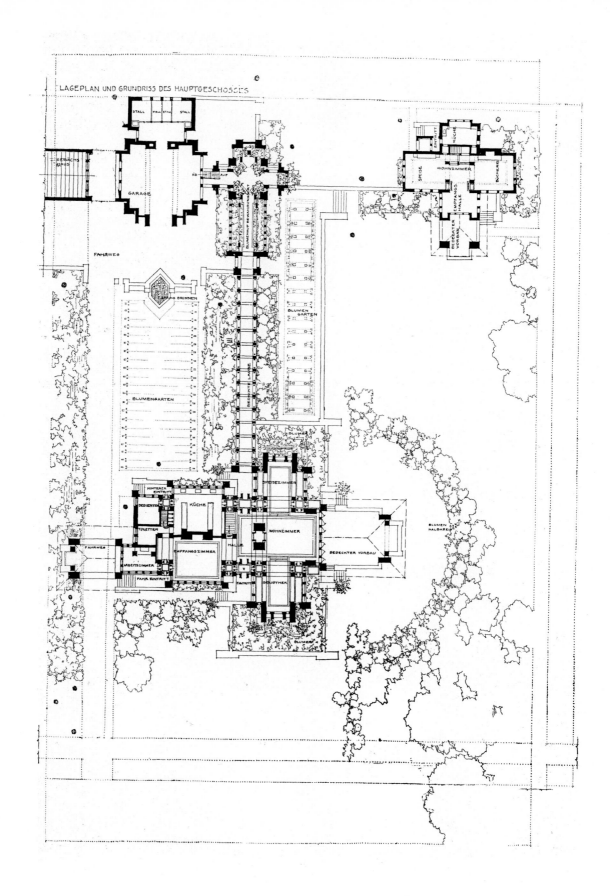

Martin house, Buffalo, N.Y. Ground plan of the main floor.

D. D. Martin house, Buffalo, N.Y. Bird's-eye view.

D. D. Martin house, Buffalo, N.Y.

D. D. Martin house, Buffalo, N.Y. Heating unit with lighting fixture; conservatory.

Martin house, Buffalo, N.Y. Pergola and entrance hall.

Martin house, Buffalo, N.Y. Conservatory and birdhouse.

Martin house, Buffalo, N.Y. Fireplace in the living room.

Martin house, Buffalo, N.Y. Reception hall and dining room.

Martin house, Buffalo, N.Y. West facade and detail of the west facade.

Martin house, Buffalo, N.Y. Living room with heating unit and lighting fixtures.

Martin house, Buffalo, N.Y.

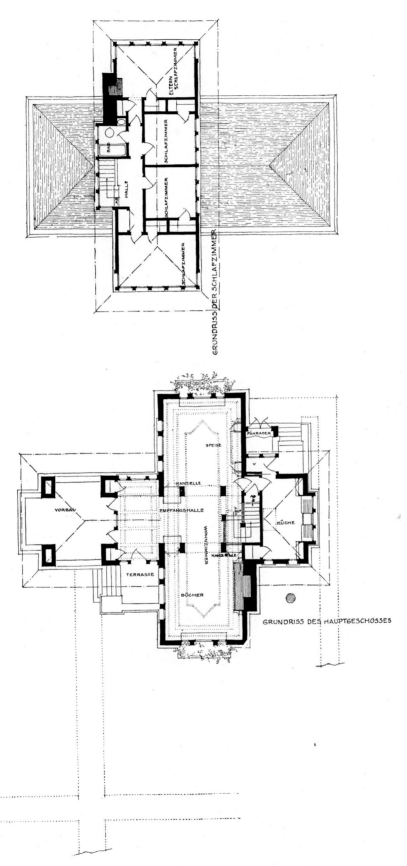

GRUNDRISS DER SCHLAFZIMMER

ELTERN SCHLAFZIMMER

SCHLAFZIMMER

SCHLAFZIMMER

SCHLAFZIMMER

BAD

HALLE

SPEISE

FAHRRADER

KANZELLE

EMPFANGSHALLE

VORBAU

WOHNZIMM

KÜCHE

KANZELLE

TERRASSE

BÜCHER

GRUNDRISS DES HAUPTGESCHOSSES

Martin house, Buffalo, N.Y. Ground plans of the main and upper floors.

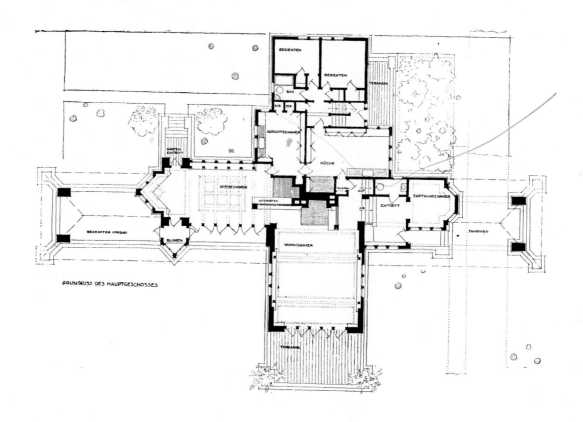

GRUNDRISS DES HAUPTGESCHOSSES

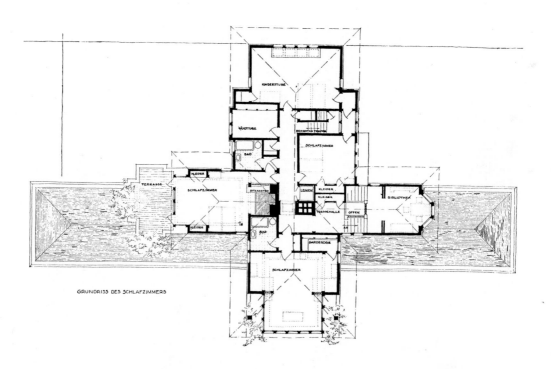

GRUNDRISS DES SCHLAFZIMMERS

Ward W. Willits house, Highland Park, Ill. Ground plans of the main and
upper floors.

Ward W. Willits house, Highland Park, Ill., 1903.

Ward W. Willits house, Highland Park, Ill. Street facade.

Ward W. Willits house, Highland Park, Ill. Entrance wing and living room.

Oscar Steffens house, Birchwood, Ill., 1909.

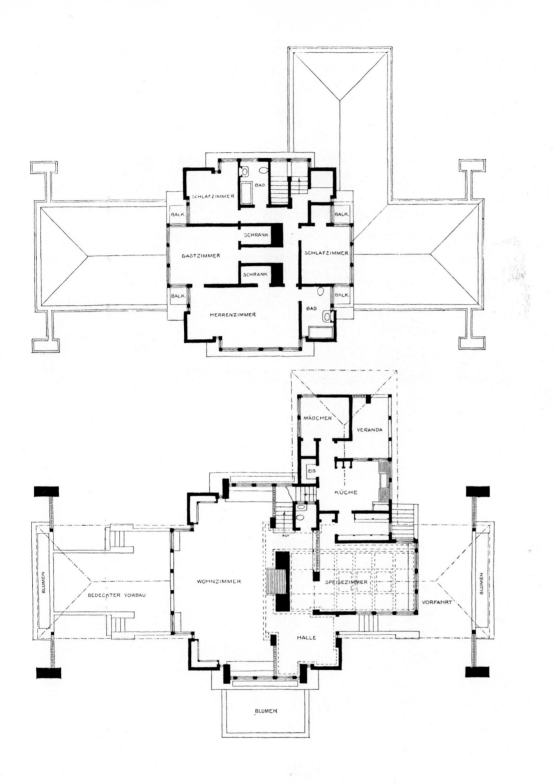

Oscar Steffens house, Birchwood, Ill. Ground plans of the main and upper
floors.

Horner house, Birchwood, Ill., 1908. Exterior, and interior facing the
entrance.

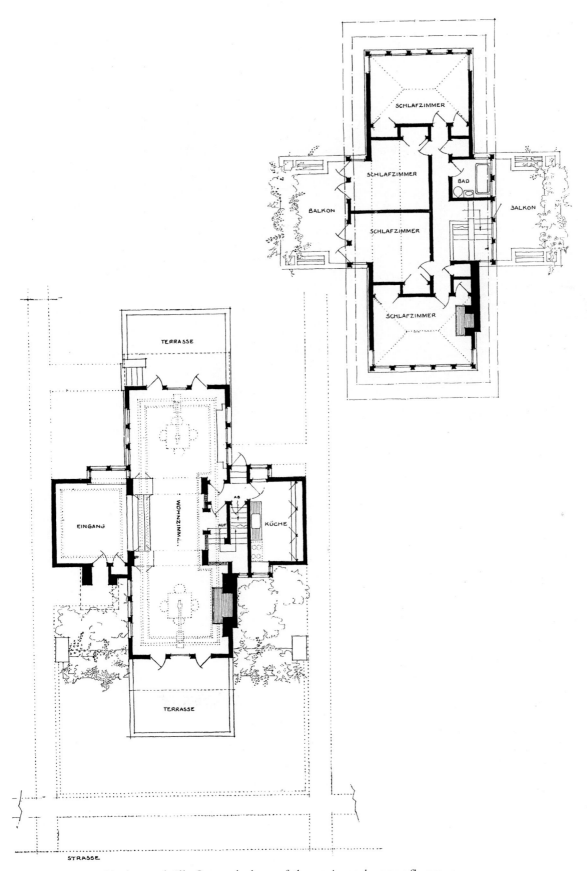

Horner house, Birchwood, Ill. Ground plans of the main and upper floors.

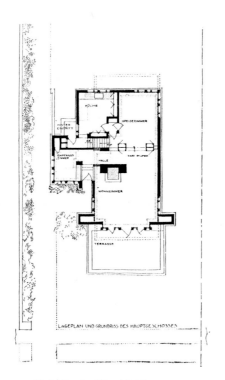

Gale house, Oak Park, Ill., 1909.

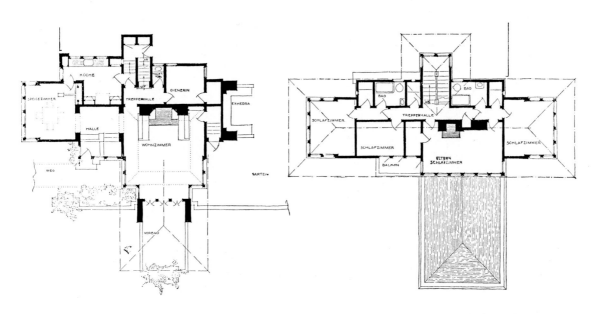

Suburban house of George Millard, Highland Park, 1906.

Country house of Isabel Roberts, River Forest, Ill., 1908.

Country house of Isabel Roberts, River Forest, Ill. South facade and living
room.

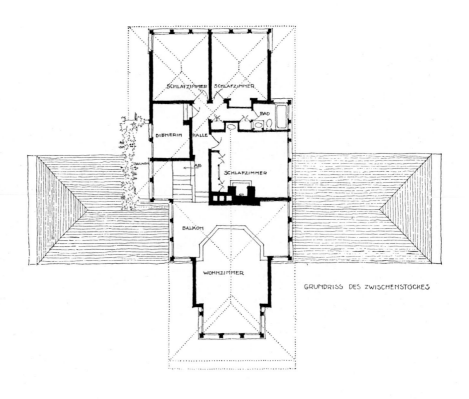

GRUNDRISS DES ZWISCHENSTÖCKES

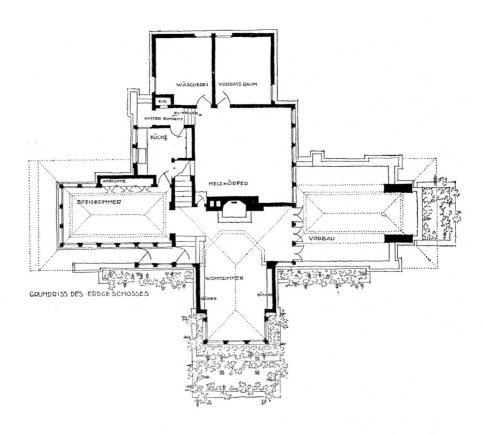

GRUNDRISS DES ERDGESCHOSSES

Country house of Isabel Roberts, River Forest, Ill. Ground plans of the main and upper floors.

Martin villa, Oak Park, Ill., 1904. Garden facade.

Tomek villa, Riverside, Ill., 1907. Street (south) facade.

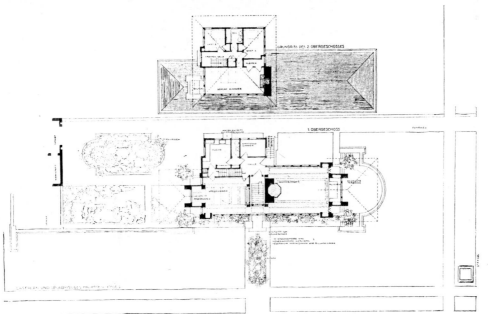

Tomek villa, Riverside, Ill. Porch and ground plan.

Emma Martin house, Oak Park, Ill., 1901.

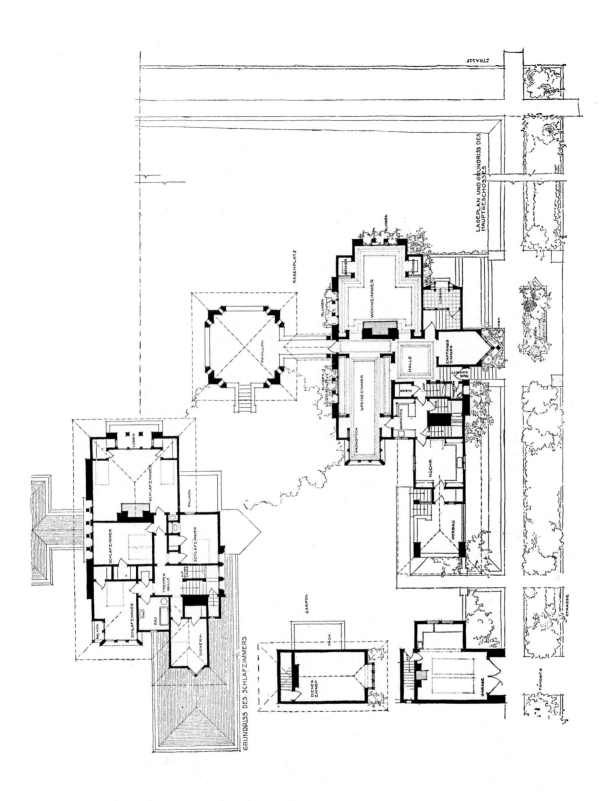

Emma Martin house, Oak Park, Ill. Ground plans of the main and upper floors.

Emma Martin house, Oak Park, Ill. Pavilion and garden facades.

Emma Martin house, Oak Park, Ill. Street facade.

Beachy villa, Oak Park, Ill. Garden facade.

Beachy villa, Oak Park, Ill. Garden and street facades.

City residence of W. R. Heath, Buffalo, N.Y., 1903.

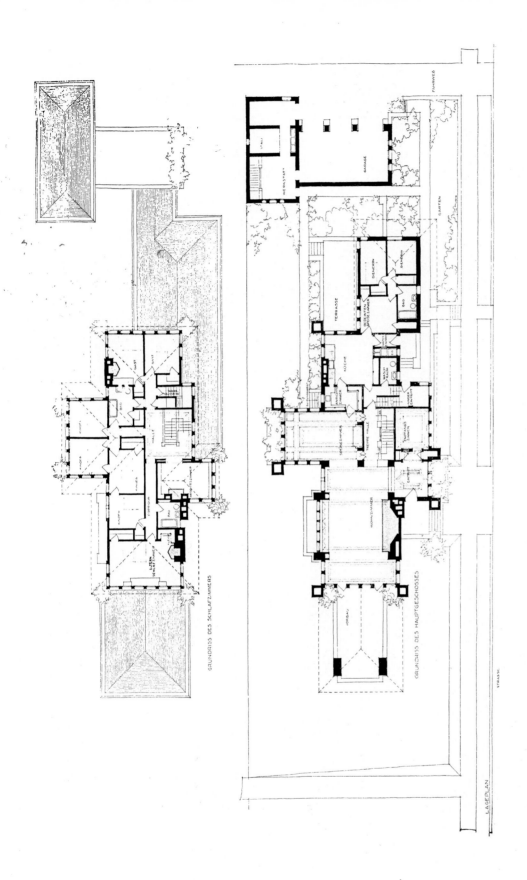

City residence of W. R. Heath, Buffalo, N.Y. Ground plans of the main and
upper floors.

City residence of W. R. Heath, Buffalo, N.Y. Details of the entrance facade.

City residence of W. R. Heath, Buffalo, N.Y. Living room.

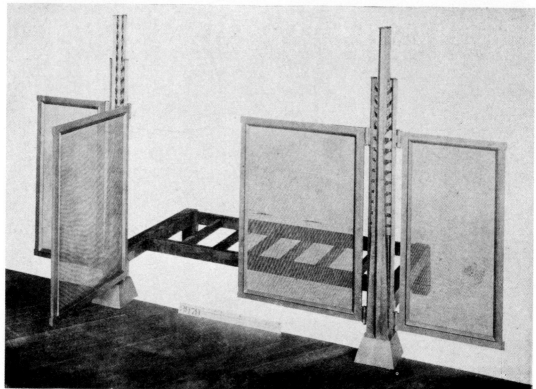

ABOVE: Heath house, Buffalo, N.Y. Fireplace. BELOW: Dana villa. Fire screen.

ABOVE: Evans house. Fireplace in the living room. BELOW: Bradley villa. Fireplace in the living room.

Suburban house of Robert Evans, Longwood, Ill., 1909.

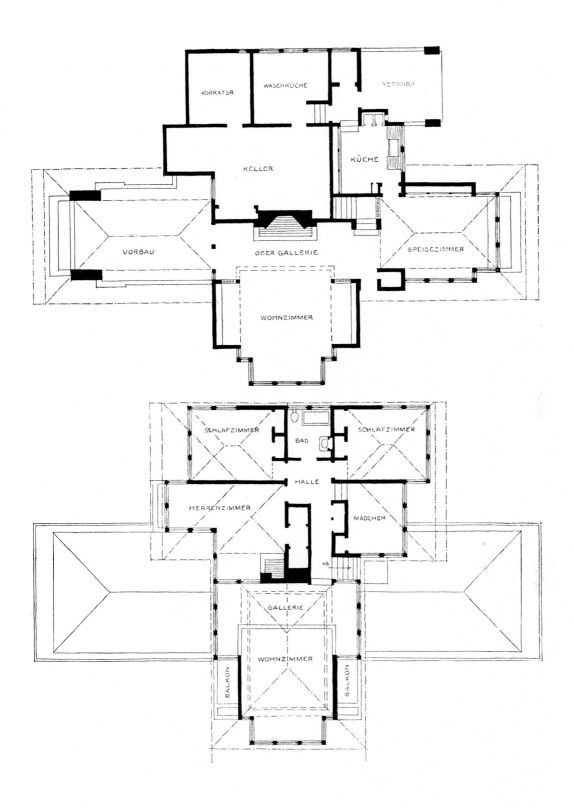

Suburban house of Robert Evans, Longwood, Ill. Ground plans of the main
   and upper floors.

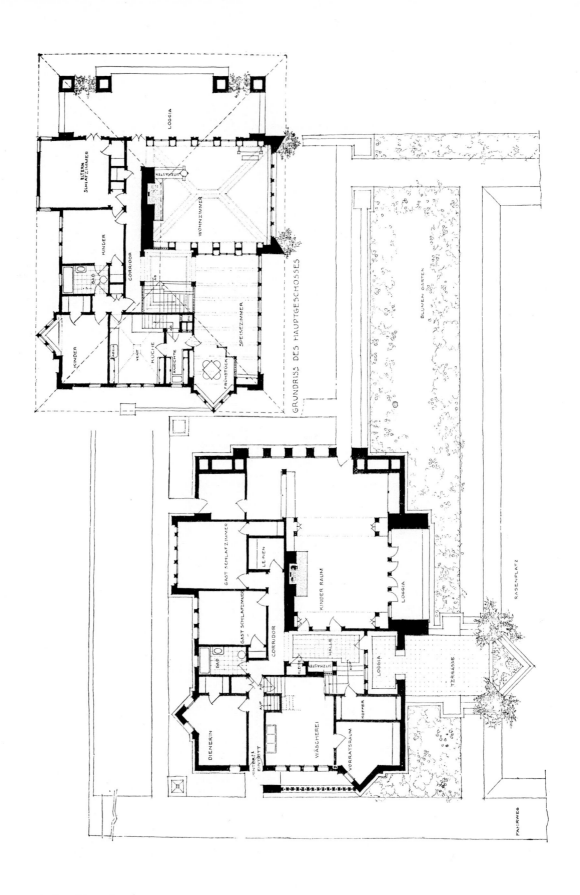

Arthur Heurtley house, Oak Park, Ill., 1901. Ground plans of the main and
upper floors.

Arthur Heurtley house, Oak Park, Ill. Street facade and upper hall.

Arthur Heurtley house, Oak Park, Ill. North and south facades.

Arthur Heurtley house, Oak Park, Ill. Street facade.

Meyer May house, Grand Rapids, Mich. Fireplace in the living room; dining room.

Meyer May house, Grand Rapids, Mich., 1909.

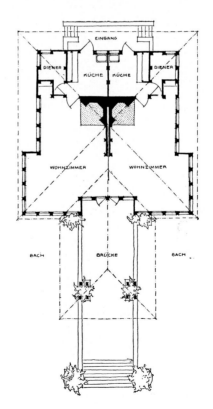

Twin summer house of George E. Gerts, Birch Brooks, Mich.

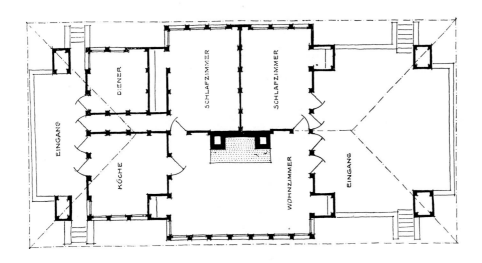

Summer house of Walter Gerts, Birch Brook, Mich., 1902.

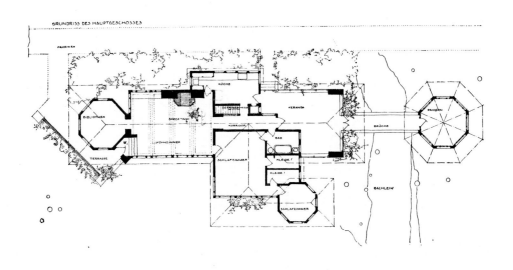

Country house of W. A. Glasner, Glencoe, Ill.

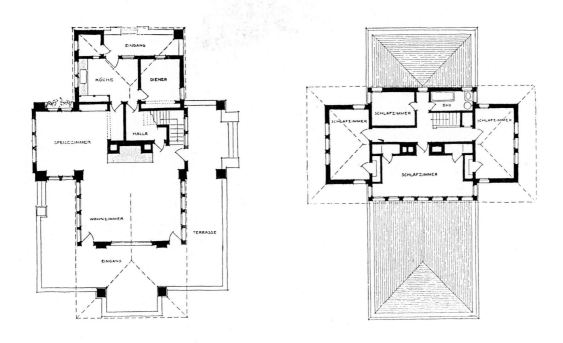

Summer house of Charles Ross, Lake Delavan, Wis.

Frank J. Baker villa, Witmeth, Ill., 1909. Street facade.

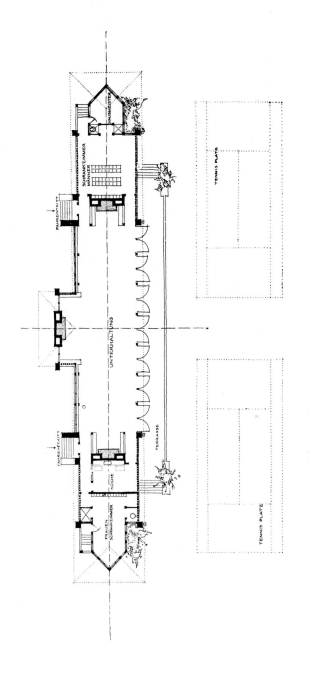

River Forest Tennis Club, River Forest, Ill., 1906.

Frank Lloyd Wright studio. Portrait figure, Richard Bock, sculptor.

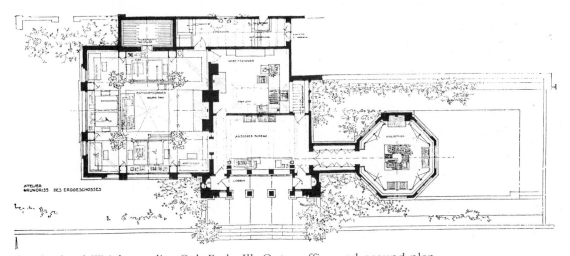

Frank Lloyd Wright studio, Oak Park, Ill. Outer office and ground plan.

Browne's bookstore. Fine Arts Buildings, Chicago, 1907.

Special exhibition of drawings and models in the Chicago Art Institute,
  Chicago, 1907.

Special exhibition of drawings and models in the Chicago Art Institute, Chicago, 1907.

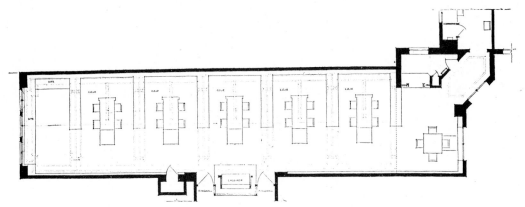

ABOVE: Special exhibition of drawings and models in the Chicago Art Institute, Chicago, Ill. BELOW: Browne's bookstore, Chicago, Ill. Ground plan.

ABOVE: Browne's bookstore, Chicago, Ill. Detail. BELOW: Frank Lloyd Wright
    studio, Oak Park, Ill. Detail of the entrance.

ABOVE: Browne's bookstore, Chicago, Ill. Cashier's counter. BELOW: Frank
Lloyd Wright studio, Chicago, Ill. Entrance.

ABOVE: Browne's bookstore, Chicago, Ill. Detail. BELOW: Frank Lloyd Wright studio, Chicago, Ill. Library.

Browne's bookstore, Chicago, Ill. Display window and entrance; reading room.

Frank Lloyd Wright studio, Chicago, Ill. Workroom.

Thurber exhibition gallery for paintings and etchings.

Martin house, Buffalo, N.Y. Fireplace wall in gold-glass mosaic.

Exhibition at Madison Square Garden, New York, 1910. Design carried out
   in cement and tiles.

City residence of Fred C. Robie, Chicago, Ill., 1906. Woodlawn Ave. South facade.

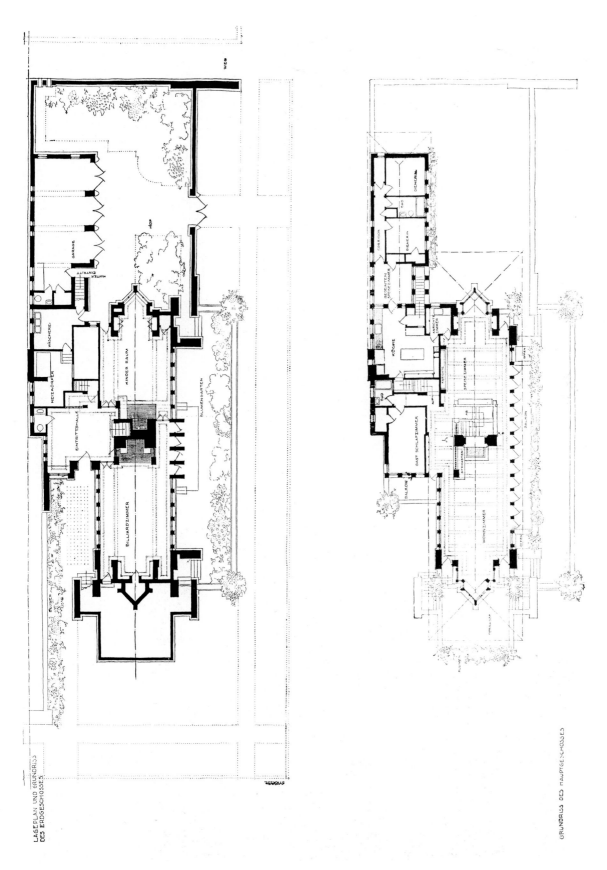

LAGEPLAN UND GRUNDRISS
DES ERDGESCHOSSES.

GRUNDRISS DES HAUPTGESCHOSSES.

City residence of Fred C. Robie, Chicago, Ill. Ground plans of the main and
  upper floors.

Robie house, Chicago, Ill. Fireplace; living room. In the ceiling is an electrically illuminated skylight framed with laths.

Robie house, Chicago, Ill. Dining room.

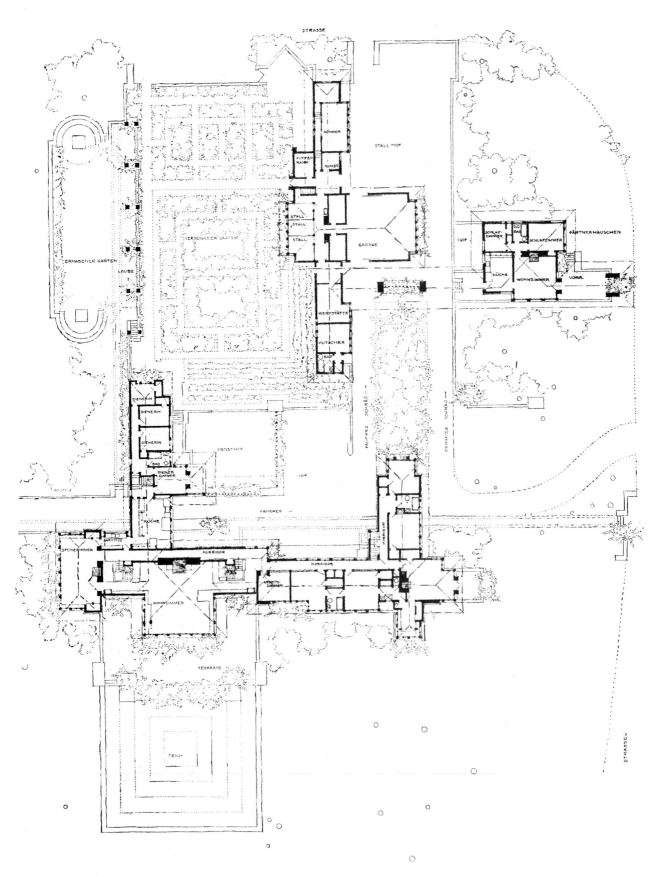

Avery Coonley house, Riverside, Ill., 1908. Ground plan.

Avery Coonley house, Riverside, Ill. Living-room wing and terrace.

Avery Coonley house, Riverside, Ill. Dining-room, living-room and bedroom
wings, joined by galleries.

Avery Coonley house, Riverside, Ill. Details.

Avery Coonley house, Riverside, Ill. Master-bedroom and guest-room wings.

Avery Coonley house, Riverside, Ill. Galleries with skylight, the living room
in the middle; dressing room.

Avery Coonley house, Riverside, Ill. Detail of the terrace.

Avery Coonley house, Riverside, Ill. Inner and entrance courts (walls with
facing of colored tiles).

Avery Coonley house, Riverside, Ill. Fireplace in the living room; master-bedroom, dressing-room and guest-room wings.

Avery Coonley house, Riverside, Ill. Living room with a view through the gallery toward the dining room; in the living room, an electrically illuminated skylight, framed with laths.

Avery Coonley house, Riverside, Ill. General view.

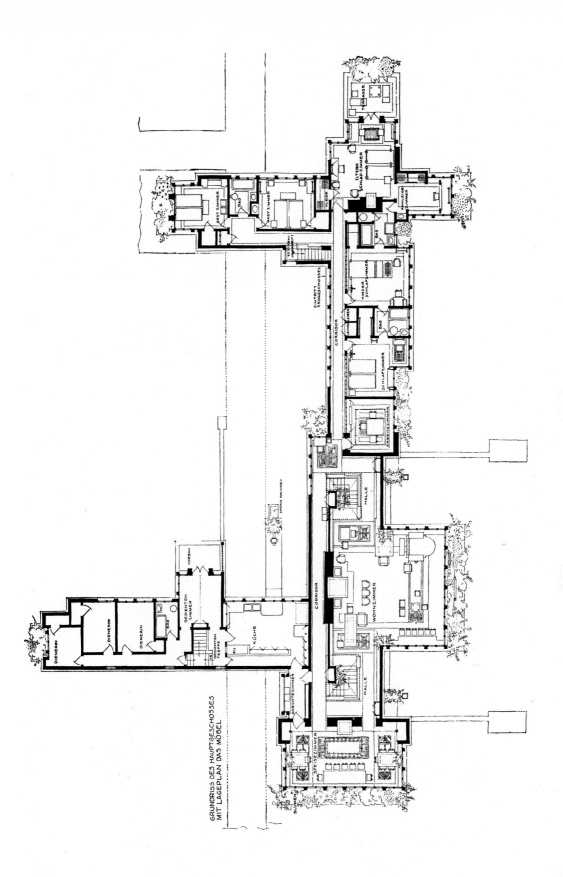

Avery Coonley house, Riverside, Ill. Ground plan of the main floor.

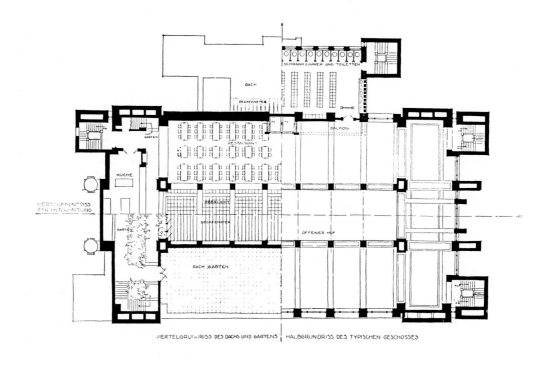

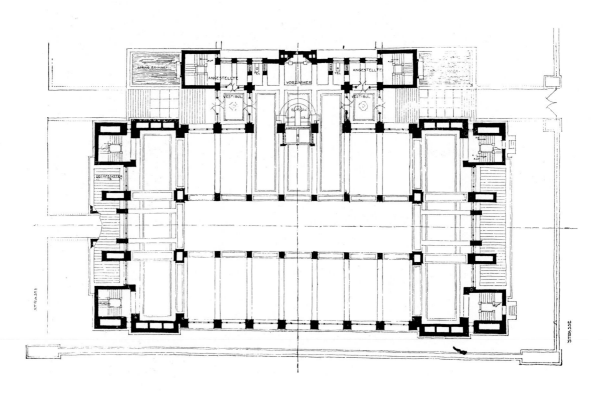

Administration building of the Larkin factories, Buffalo, N.Y. Ground plans.

Administration building of the Larkin factories, Buffalo, N.Y., 1903.

Administration building of the Larkin factories, Buffalo, N.Y. Central hall.

Administration building of the Larkin factories, Buffalo, N.Y. The front from
  Seneca Street.

Administration building of the Larkin factories, Buffalo, N.Y. Partial view of the upper gallery. Executed in brick, magnesite slabs and metal.

Administration building of the Larkin factories, Buffalo, N.Y. View of the director's room and the administration rooms; information desk in the entrance hall. Executed in brick, magnesite slabs and metal.

Administration building of the Larkin factories, Buffalo, N.Y. View of an office.
Furniture of metal and magnesite slabs.

Administration building of the Larkin factories, Buffalo, N.Y. Fountain at the entrance side, and details.

Administration building of the Larkin factories, Buffalo, N.Y. View of a floor
  at work and closed down.

Administration building of the Larkin factories, Buffalo, N.Y. Examples of the furnishings of the office. Double window with metal frames, metal furniture, and metal correspondence files under the windows.

Administration building of the Larkin factories, Buffalo, N.Y. Typical
arrangement of a floor with a view toward the central hall.

Administration building of the Larkin factories, Buffalo, N.Y. Entrance to the
employees' clubroom, and gallery with writing desks for callers.

Administration building of the Larkin factories, Buffalo, N.Y. Front on Seneca Street.